This book is dedicated to all who find Nature not an adversary to conquer and destroy, but a storehouse of infinite knowledge and experience linking man to all things past and present. They know conserving the natural environment is essential to our future well-being.

CAPE COD
THE STORY BEHIND THE SCENERY®

by Glen Kaye

Glen Kaye, career professional with the National Park Service, has served the public for many years in the interpretation of parks from Hawaii to New England. In his tenure as chief park naturalist at Cape Cod National Seashore, he gained an intimate perception and fine appreciation of the special world that is Cape Cod. Glen, a graduate of Oregon State University, is also the author of *Hawaii Volcanoes*, another in *The Story Behind the Scenery* series.

Front cover: Herring gull; photo by Lynn M. Stone. Inside cover, pages 2–3: Scallop shell, beach near Highland Light; photos by Glenn Van Nimwegen. This page: Common tern; NPS photo.

Book Design by K. C. DenDooven

Second Printing, 1987

The sea has many voices. Listen to the surf, really lend it your ears, and you will hear in it a world of sounds. . . . [a] great sound . . . constantly changing its tempo, its pitch, its accent, and its rhythm . . . now almost placid . . . now grave and solemn-slow . . . now a rhythm monstrous with a sense of purpose and elemental will.

—HENRY BESTON, *The Outermost House*

Cape Cod: A sea-washed, windblown arm of land jutting from the coast of Massachusetts. A trailing ribbon of picturesque villages and clapboard cottages. A postcard view of wheeling gulls, lonely lighthouses, wave-tossed sails. And a symbol, a window on America's past.

For it is largely here that America, as we know it, began. Whether our ancestors arrived on the *Mayflower* or entered through the thronging portals of Ellis Island and the like, the sights and sounds of Cape Cod evoke a heritage that belongs to us all. Remnants of farms and relics of windmills and fishermen's shacks tell us how necessity was met by ingenuity. Winding streets take us to steepled churches and to crowded graveyards that reveal poignant stories in their crumbling headstones. And cranberry bogs remind us of that long-ago season of Thanksgiving, when Indian and Pilgrim made the first, if uneasy, overtures that would eventually grow into a new meaning of brotherhood for all the world.

For a few fleeting moments we walk in that centuries-old world of the Pilgrims, the English architects of our society. And although their ways seem simple and sometimes absurdly quaint to us now, we are filled with awe and respect for these first American pioneers, who faced unbelievable hardship and the yawning unknown—all for the sake of personal dignity and a principle. Would *we* have had such courage, such conviction, such faith and foresight? We wonder!

Cape Cod, then, stirs our emotions with nostalgia and a deepening appreciation of our New England heritage. This would be enough for most of us, but at Cape Cod we are given a bonus at every turn. For nature here is generous with her gifts: hammering surf and bright beaches, fragile blossoms and wind-sculpted dunes and a variety of birds that come and go with the seasons in a never-ending pageant of ineffable grace.

Small wonder that this beautiful and historic place is a protected area! But we are fortunate that a few years ago a few people had the faith, foresight, and conviction to work for its preservation. And the courage. For by then this was not just a few acres of remote wilderness. It was a fast-developing land, well on its way toward joining the long line of pristine beaches wasted in the consuming stampede of civilization.

Courage? Conviction? Faith and foresight? Perhaps we are not so far removed, after all, from those searchers who stood on these very shores—the beaches of Cape Cod National Seashore—well over three centuries ago!—G.D.D.

JEFF MYERS/H. ARMSTRONG ROBERTS INC.

It is the great, upraised "arm" of Cape Cod that captures the imagination: Like a gigantic human limb outlined by the sea, an "elbow" juts eastward for a distance of about forty miles from the mainland, a "forearm" extends northward forty miles more, a half-curled "hand" arcs gracefully back upon the mainland in an ever-tightening curve and terminates in tapering, wave-built "fingers" of sand.

The Cape

This is a fresh, young landscape, as geologic features go. It was created largely by glaciers during the last ice age and then was given its most recent shape by waves and the rising sea. But however young the features we see here now may be, they are only the latest chapter in a geologic story that reaches beneath the surface of the land and the surrounding sea and stretches into the impenetrable past. Whole chapters of the story are missing, but still surviving are fragments of earth that provide us with a few paragraphs telling of the ancient precursors of Cape Cod, Martha's Vineyard, and Nantucket. The ancestral landscapes that were the foundation for today's landscape resembled but little the scene before us. Someday, this landscape too will fade away, with the relentless passage of time, and a new one will take its place.

THE FOUNDATION

None of the exposed cape is "solid" rock. It is built entirely of debris that was transported here by wind and water and ice. Only if one drills deep enough—three hundred to five hundred feet—will one encounter the granitic bedrock of the continent that is so readily exposed elsewhere in Massachusetts.

This basement rock dates back to a time that is incomprehensible in its antiquity. It is evidence of profound change, for North America was once connected with Europe, Asia, and Africa in the supercontinent geologists refer to as *Pangaea*. This gray granite was joined to the identical granite of what is today Morocco, in northern Africa. But about 200 million years ago, the continents began to separate, in a slow, wrenching motion. This motion continues today, a process that is known as *continental drift,* or *plate tectonics.*

Both before and after continental separation occurred, this part of North America was subjected to a complex history. Mountains were uplifted and eroded, sediments were deposited, volcanic rocks were exposed, and rocks—after millions of years of incredible pressure—were

This peat bank on the Great Beach is symbolic of the constant change taking place at Cape Cod. A product of salt marshes, it now lies out of its element, exposed and vulnerable to the assault of eroding waves.

altered into metamorphic rock called *gneisses* and *schists.* It is on such bedrock that the visible record begins. From this point, the story becomes one of deposition and erosion, caused by the repeated rising and falling of the seas for the hundred million years that preceded the coming of the glaciers.

BUILDING SEDIMENTS

From the flowing streams of northeastern mountains, debris extended eastward, eventually reaching into the seas of the Cretaceous period. Great deposits of sand and silt covered the bedrock so that, as the oceans rose, a land of deltas and swamps was created.

The Cretaceous was the age of trees and flowering plants: Sequoia and pine grew here, as did holly and oak and willow, magnolia and sassafras. Century after century, the sediment of the organic-filled swamps grew thicker.

Slowly the rising seas flooded this land of deltas and swamps, and fine mud from the rivers buried under hundreds of feet of sediment the peaty swamps that once had been forests. With the passing of time and the increase of pressure, the mud became clay, and lignite was formed from the accumulated forest products. Much of that clay is gone now, scoured away by the glaciers, but both clay and low-grade coal are still evident on Martha's Vineyard, the oldest strata that are still visible in the region. These same ninety-five- to seventy-million-year-old deposits probably extend into the sedimentary layers that lie beneath Nantucket and Cape Cod.

"Butter-and-eggs"

For the next seventy million years—the Tertiary period—the ancient seas fell and rose and fell again. Coastal New England was subjected to a repetitive sequence that included erosion, the growth of forests and swamps, flooding, the accumulation of marine-fossil sediments, exposure, and again erosion. As a part of this process, more swamp-formed peat was buried and converted into yet another layer of carbonaceous material. This deposit lies under Cape Cod, beneath the sands of Provincetown.

Exposed at last, the Cretaceous and Tertiary sediments became another coastal plain, this time eroded into a chain of distinctively shaped hills running parallel to the coast. The position of this chain is notable, for these hills would be the resting ground for the glaciers to come and would thus allow the highest glacial debris to stand above the ocean, today's Cape Cod and associated islands.

THE ADVANCE OF THE ICE

Ice has been the most significant of all the landshaping processes by which nature has molded the earth over the past two million years. So remarkable were the achievements of the glaciers that these events have been grouped together into one unit of geologic time: the Pleistocene epoch, commonly referred to as the "Ice Age." The ice has spread across northern latitudes at least seven times in the last 700 thousand years. But it was only twenty-six thousand to twenty thousand years ago—during the deepest of the Wisconsin stage of glaciation—that the ice

The slender trunks of red maple saplings stretch from a sun-dappled forest floor. A brilliant element in Cape Cod's distinctive autumns, the red maple grows only in moist areas such as this swamp.

reached this region and altered it to produce the major features exhibited here today.

These were the continental ice sheets, created from accumulations of unmelted snow so deep that at last they coalesced into ice and began to slowly spread from their points of origin. Labrador was the source of the ice sheets that covered central and eastern North America.

The ice sheets were so enormous as to defy description. They towered perhaps two miles high and covered millions of square miles of land. The power of the moving ice, with such a massive weight behind it, was irresistible. As long as the Labradorean source continued to be fed by snow, the ice would advance.

The ice sheets pushed their way inexorably southward, plucking rocks from their resting places. These rocks became glacial tools with which the glacier scoured and gouged the earth into great valleys and plains. Armed with these cutting edges, the ice sheets carved the glacial striations found all across New England, documenting for us the routes they took.

The first glacial advance barely extended this far south. Yet, during a minor retreat in which the water that had been entrapped as ice melted and covered the land with a warm interglacial sea, some twenty-five feet of mud settled—mud that is now most evident as a blue-gray clay on Martha's Vineyard and beneath Highland Light.

The next advance of the ice left a greater legacy, since it built much of the mass that forms the Cape and associated islands. Alternating layers of glacial debris and marine clay were also laid down during this advance, proving that minor fluctuations in the ice front and the level of the sea did take place. The earthen bands that reveal these changes are exposed in the cliff of the Great Beach, most notably at Nauset Light.

The third glacial advance at this latitude happened only a geologic "second" ago, somewhere between 23,000 and 16,000 B.C. Of the three glacial advances, we know the most about this one—because it was the latest, of course, and because it was deformed the least by subsequent events.

At its greatest extent, the scalloped edge of the glacial sheet lay south of what is now Rhode Island and across the land we know as Martha's Vineyard and Nantucket. Part of the ice sheet lay to the east and extended just as far south. The ice along this great glacial front stalled, as melting and advancement balanced one another for a time. Meanwhile, in conveyor-belt fashion, the glacier carried forward its scrapings of boulders and gravel, sand, rock powder, and organic debris, giving them up at its wasting terminus. This was the pattern of deposition that began the building of the distinctive features we see here today.

To the west, morainal debris from the edge of the Buzzard's Bay lobe of the ice sheet erected

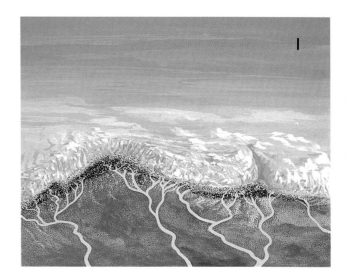

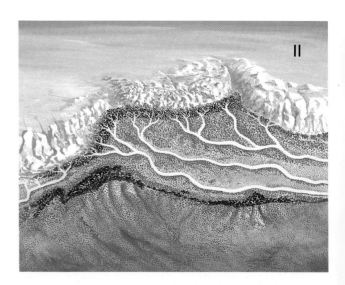

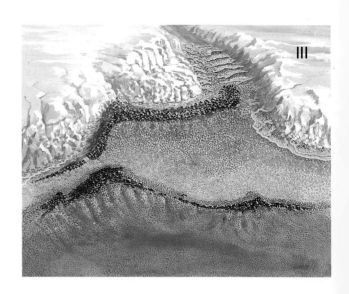

what is now the northwestern side of Martha's Vineyard. The Cape Cod Bay lobe adjacent to it built the northeastern side of Martha's Vineyard and the northern side of Nantucket. To the east, the South Channel lobe also piled its debris, now eroded remnants that are either obscured by the sea or evident only as shoals.

As the climate of the earth warmed, the ice began its final, erratic retreat northward. But once again the glacier stalled; again a temporary balance was maintained; again the ice lobes piled up their earthen burdens. This was when the Buzzard's Bay lobe built the morainal ridge that is now the Elizabeth Islands and the western end of Cape Cod; and it was when the Cape Cod Bay lobe piled (between Sandwich and Orleans) the morainal debris that now forms the "biceps" of Cape Cod.

All the while, torrents of water were pouring southward from the deteriorating ice front. In these meltwater streams, small pieces of glacial debris were carried forth and deposited on the gradually sloping outwash plains associated with each moraine. These plains now form the southern side of Martha's Vineyard and Nantucket and also form the "triceps" of Cape Cod between Falmouth and Chatham.

In the same manner, a fistless "forearm," from "elbow" to "wrist," was laid down as meltwater from continued glacial retreat swept outwash debris from both the Cape Cod Bay lobe to the west and the South Channel lobe to the east. The glacial waters remained for a time, a condition that added clay-forming sediments to the growing forearm.

In an outwash plain such as this, the absence of large boulders is as conspicuous as is their prevalence in the regions of glacial moraines. Running water could not move heavy boulders for any significant distance, but the action of

Olympian views illustrate the ice-age processes that shaped Cape Cod: The great continental glacier developed a stabilized front (I), whereon countless tons of earthen debris were deposited (now the high points of Martha's Vineyard and Nantucket). Glacial retreat and a second stabilized front (II) allowed debris to build the nascent Elizabeth Islands and the bicep of Cape Cod. Then meltwaters carried fine glacial debris (III) into the area of Cape Cod's future forearm. About five thousand years ago, a higher sea level covered the lowlands (IV); erosion had yet to smooth the coastline and create the sand spits of today.

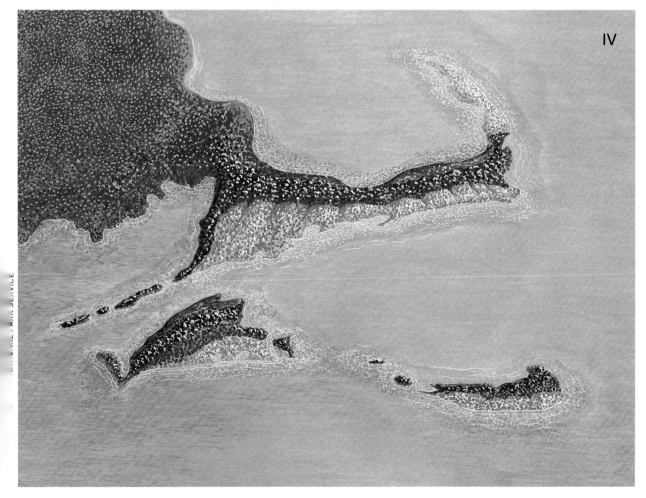

DAVID COATES

Lush vegetation accents the rounded contours of Great Pond. Lying remarkably close to the sea, kettle ponds are freshwater pockets that were lifted as the sea rose following glacier melt.

A fresh storm breach in Monomoy Island dramatically demonstrates the tenuousness of the equilibrium existing between barrier beaches and the sea. Chatham, at the elbow of Cape Cod, lies to the north.

little more than a thousand years the ice front melted back a distance of at least a hundred miles!

As this new landscape was exposed, it exhibited distinctive features, evident today:

Kettles: great depressions that mark the places where huge blocks of stagnating ice once lay. When these blocks, which were partly or completely buried by outwash debris, melted, they left craterlike cavities that vary in size up to a half-mile in diameter.

Kames: cone-shaped mounds of outwash debris.

Erratics: boulders that were picked up by the glacier and deposited some distance from their point of origin. They are usually found on moraines and are often seen in the stone fences that were constructed by pioneering farmers on the land they cleared for cultivation.

Pamets: irregularly contoured outwash channels that were carved while the ground yet contained stagnant ice.

Still the Cape, as we know it, did not exist. The ice had receded, but a vast amount of water —eight or nine million *cubic miles*—remained tied up in the great glacial sheets of the world, so that the oceans stood some four hundred feet lower than they do today. If a viewer had been present at the time, he would have seen what was to be Cape Cod, Nantucket, and Martha's Vineyard as only the highest areas of a great, glacier-produced landscape.

A moraine lay exposed where Cape Cod Bay would form, and other moraines lay to the south (beyond Nantucket). The great expanse that would become Georges Bank also lay exposed as a morainal rise, and it extended about 150 miles southeastward from present-day Chatham before sloping into the Pleistocene sea.

the glacial waters had other effects that are still apparent. For example, at Truro, Wellfleet, and Eastham the outwash debris slopes downhill from the east to the west and southwest, the same directions in which water flowed and debris was transported. Also extending from the ocean to the bay are various "hollows," former drainage channels that were filled with water when the South Channel lobe melted.

If the rate of glacial retreat is a valid gauge, the speed at which the final construction of all of these moraines and outwash plains took place must have been phenomenal. Using radiocarbon dating, tundra plants at Martha's Vineyard have been found to be about 15,300 years old, and marine clays at Boston 14,000 years old. Thus in

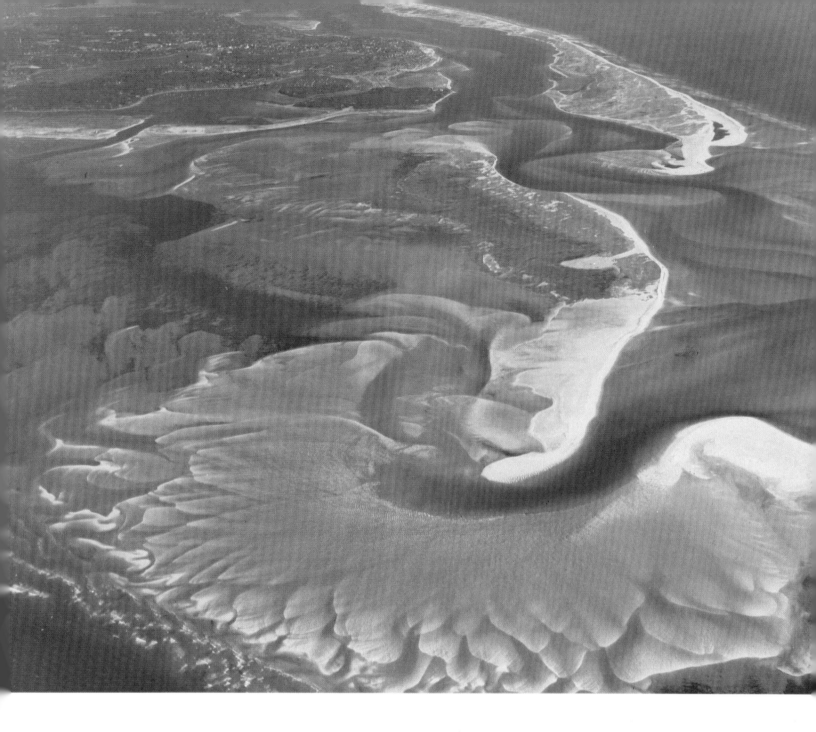

The Rise and Attack of the Sea

As the glacier retreated, the melting waters joined the sea, which at last began to rise. The recently exposed lands were slowly drowned. Georges Bank came into being and other high lands were reduced to shoals as the waves readily carved away the loose, unconsolidated debris they met at each level, a process that continues to this day.

But it was not until about six thousand years ago that the water reached high enough to erode the highest lands. The cliffs of Cape Cod, Nantucket, and Martha's Vineyard are products of this recent erosion. Using their rates of retreat, we can make some rough calculations as to the extent of former lands:

Within Cape Cod Bay, the cliffs are eroding at the rate of about one foot each year. On the Great Beach, facing eastward to the ocean, the cliffs of the Lower Cape are retreating by about three feet each year. These average rates have been recorded over the past century, and in all likelihood erosion proceeded at these same rates during prehistoric time. If so, then a much fatter forearm once existed, one that extended some two miles to the east and possessed an irregular coastline.

What happened to all this material? Much of it was carried offshore beyond the action of the waves, where it was dispersed as marine sediment on the ocean floor. Some of it simply dissolved in the sea. And much of it was transported and reshaped into new land.

How is soil-and-rock debris transported from one place on shore to another? Waves rather than currents are the driving force in this process,

At Highland Light, Truro, the coastline is rapidly retreating. The life span of many Lower Cape structures is measurable; by pacing off the distance from the cliff edge, one can closely predict the number of years until a building's demise.

called *longshore transport*. They rework the material of the cliffs onto the beach, stir it up, suspend it temporarily, then move it up or down the coast at the same angle at which the breakers strike the land. The long-term direction of the waves, then, determines the long-term direction of the movement of sand. Since the winter storms that strike Cape Cod typically arrive from the northeast, the sands of Truro are usually swept northward; those of Wellfleet, Eastham, and Orleans are driven south.

Volume is significant. On the Great Beach, for example, about 459,000 cubic yards of coastal debris are jostled and swirled northward past any one point each year, and about 230,000 cubic yards of material are moved south. In this process, sand spits—some of the youngest geologic features of Cape Cod—have extended from every irregularity of land, and they are still growing.

Curving from the glacial cliffs of Truro, which feed it, is the great "fist" of Provincetown, the most dramatic and the youngest of these sand

spits. Its creation began some six thousand years ago. After Georges Bank was submerged, easterly winds drove the great waves against the now unprotected land with the full force of their power. Chatham's Nauset Beach and Monomoy Island (sometimes called "Monomoy Spit") were also created by longshore transport, in these cases fed by the eroding cliffs to the north.

The rising sea created another distinctive feature in today's landscape—the ponds. None of these ponds existed when the glacial lobes retreated. Rainwater quickly percolated through the porous soil, and even the deepest depressions remained dry. As the level of the sea rose, however, the level of freshwater saturation beneath the land also rose, and at last the water reached the kettle holes. Today's ponds, then, are the exposed portions of that freshwater table.

The rising sea also drowned the mouths of drainage channels and created such "rivers" as the Pamet and the Bass, which in reality are *tidal-flow streams*.

The Ebb and Flow of Life

It is the nature of all forms of life to spread wherever they can and to reproduce as much as they are able. Therefore the barren landscape exposed by the retreating glaciers did not have long to wait until it was covered with the colorful clothing of life. Wave after wave of plants appeared as the climate warmed and life spread northward. The evidence? It lies, in part, in the pollen record disclosed within the twenty-foot deposit of peat in the swamps and bogs of the Cape.

The first plants to appear were northern tundra and arctic species that were tolerant of cold and could support arctic species of animals, such as the caribou. In time, as the climate became less and less severe, northern species of pines, spruces, and hemlocks established themselves, followed by the temperate plants so abundant here today: red maple, pitch pine, and black oak.

Yet the warming process was not a steady one. The climate did fluctuate. At times it was even milder than it is today, and such warmth-loving species as sycamore, chestnut, magnolia, and poplar once grew this far north. Since at least A.D. 1450, however, the climate has been cooling (worldwide), and the northern limit of these plants has been moving progressively southward.

Today, representatives of warm and cold climatic periods are a familiar part of the scenery. The bearberry, leatherleaf, golden heather, and checkerberry are among the northern species that survived the warming trend. Atlantic white cedar, tupelo, holly, and inkberry are among the southern species that endure here and there as relict populations from a warmer time.

Also, the lowered seas exposed land and thus made it available to populations of animal life. Mastodon and mammoth teeth have been dredged from the continental shelf south and east of Cape Cod. Drowned Atlantic white cedar trunks off the coast of Provincetown and Yarmouth prove that the now-vanished land was once forested and that the rise of the sea was a recent occurrence. (As recently as three thousand years ago the sea was some sixteen feet lower than it is today; eighteen hundred years ago the ocean was about seven feet below its present level.)

The rising sea flooded land and vegetation, but for the past twenty-one hundred years the *rate* of rise has slowed to about a third of a foot per century. This condition has allowed the development of great salt marshes, such as those sheltered by Barnstable's Sandy Neck and Nauset

GLENN VAN NIMWEGEN

The "typical" Cape Cod forest of today is not the scene of yesterday, nor of tomorrow. Virtually denuded as a result of heavy use by settlers, the land is still undergoing the process of recovery. First to invade barren ground in such an area is the bearberry (foreground), a tightly growing ground cover that stabilizes the earth and permits other seedlings to take root and flourish. Bear (scrub) oak is a common successor. Pitch pine also invades bearberry fields, gradually piercing and overtopping the low oak canopy. In time, perhaps another hundred years, this scene will have given way to one that features a forest of black oak and white oak.

Spit. The marshes are still expanding; they cover the low-lying, tide-touched land wherever it is protected from the direct impact of the open sea.

In the geologic sense of time, advancing life followed rapidly upon the heels of the retreating glaciers. In all likelihood, the land was well carpeted with vegetation when the first nomadic tribes appeared.

FOOTNOTES TO THE STORY

A note of caution: A story that covers 200 million years cannot be one of smooth continuity. And it cannot be one without gaps—yawning pockets of time whose contents mystify and elude us. A continuous sequence is known to us only when the record that is revealed on the land is continuous. When erosion removes this record, we are left wondering.

Nor is the story identical in any two places. A time of deposition in one place may have been a time of erosion elsewhere. It is therefore necessary to study layers that are widely separated in order to piece together a fuller story.

Still, the processes of the past do help us to predict the future. In a relatively short period, geologically speaking, Cape Cod and its associated islands will disappear, Certainly the glacial debris will continue to be worked from the cliffs and moved along the coast to build new land. (For every two acres of land removed from the Lower Cape, one acre will be added by spit development.) So the great sand spits will grow, but *only* as long as the cliffs of outwash or morainal debris exist to feed them. When these are consumed, the friable material of the sand spits gradually will be dispersed by the waves and overwhelmed by the sea.

How long will it take? A quick look at a map suggests the future. At the current rate of erosion, ocean waves could breach the lower arm of Cape Cod at its narrowest point (at South Wellfleet) in four to six thousand years.

Concern about the demise of Cape Cod, however, is unwarranted. Although the ocean is still rising and the land disappearing, there is good reason to believe that these processes will some day come to an end. Some geologists theorize that this is indeed what *will* happen; they predict that the next ice age is close at hand.

We cannot be absolutely certain of what the future holds in store for Cape Cod. But we do know that what we see on modern maps as a distinct, humanlike arm is in reality a geological curiosity of only recent creation. It is a "one-act geographical drama" that in the coming centuries will give way to another scene, a different landscape.

Boston
Weymouth
Plymouth
Provincetown
CAPE COD
Hyannis
Nantucket
Martha's Vineyard

This infrared EROS satellite photo, taken fifty-seven miles above the earth, reveals major landforms and man-made developments. Urban areas (dark patches) and even highways are evident. Barrier beaches and spits reveal accumulations of sand. The light-blue patches reveal shallow waters, areas of sand deposition or recent inundation.

SUGGESTED READING

CHAMBERLAIN, BARBARA BLAU. *These Fragile Outposts—A Geologic Look at the Cape, Martha's Vineyard, and Nantucket.* Garden City, New York: Natural History Press, 1964.

CALDER, NIGEL. "Head south with all deliberate speed: Ice may return in a few thousand years." *Smithsonian;* January, 1978.

GIESE, GRAHAM S. AND RACHEL B. *The Eroding Shores of Outer Cape Cod.* Orleans, Mass.: The Assn. for the Preservation of Cape Cod, 1974.

Geologic History of Cape Cod, Massachusetts. U.S. Geological Survey. Washington, D.C.: U.S. Govt. Printing Office, 1976.

STERLING, DOROTHY. *Our Cape Cod Salt Marshes.* Orleans, Mass.: Assn. for the Preservation of Cape Cod, 1976.

STRAHLER, ARTHUR N. *A Geologist's View of Cape Cod.* Garden City, New York: Natural History Press, 1966.

Settling a New Land

As the monumental ice sheets of the earth's last great ice age disappeared, life followed in lavish abundance, rapidly setting the scene for the most complex of its forms—mankind.

We do not know just when it was that the first people arrived here. We only know that the charred, organic fragments found in once-occupied sites in the Hudson Valley to the north-west of Cape Cod are about eight thousand years old. Continued study—and perhaps new discoveries—may allow us glimpses of a time even further back. But until then we can only speculate. The Hudson Valley people may have wandered into this area also, traversing a forested landscape that was the precursor of Cape Cod, Martha's Vineyard, and Nantucket at a time when lowered seas offered easy access.

The early peoples of Cape Cod pursued a nomadic way of life. They hunted deer, fox, and rabbit; gathered roots, acorns, and fruits; caught fish and shellfish. When provender in one area became scarce, they simply moved on to a new area where it was more readily available.

But about A.D. 500, the Cape Cod Indians learned how to farm, having found a stable food supply in yearly harvests of corn and beans and squash. Thus the Indian way of life began to change, here and over much of North America. As settlements became more permanent, a new social order emerged in which several family groups developed, each with distinctive traditions, language, and dress. By the seventeenth century, the New England area was dominated by six tribes of the extensive Algonquin-language family. These tribes banded together in a "nation" or "federation," for the purpose of protecting each other against their common enemies.

The Indians of the Cape and associated islands were the *Wampanoags*, readily distinguished from their more warlike neighbors the Narragansetts. The Wampanoag tribe was further divided into a dozen or more sub-tribes, including the *Pamets*, in the area that is now Truro; the *Nausets*, of Eastham; and the *Monomoyicks*, of Chatham. They usually settled along creeks, marshes, and bayside shores—or wherever water and marine foods were available. There they built their homes, domed houses covered with bark or grass or reeds.

The tribe was guided in its day-to-day activities by a *sachem*, or chief. The sachem in turn was governed by a council of the bravest of the young men and the wisest of the old, the noble *sagamores*. In religious matters the Wampanoags worshiped the deity *Kiehtan*, creator of all things of the sky and earth.

The men hunted and fished, and the women tended the crops, using wood or quahog spades to till the earth. The success of every individual was important to the tribe as a whole: Since all

Once nearly gone from the landscape, the herring gull—aloof and droll—has staged a comeback on Cape Cod.

LYNN M. STONE

The Mayflower II, *floating monument to a national heritage, rides at anchor in Plymouth Harbor, where she hosts visitors in search of a link with their past. The lines of this modern replica represent an educated guess of the shape of the first* Mayflower, *which served as a wine transport before being pressed into service for its historic six weeks' voyage to the New World. The fate of the original* Mayflower *was unknown until recently, when pieces of her famous hulk surfaced in a barn near London!*

White water lily, emblem of purity, graces a freshwater pond.

LYNN M. STONE

We usually think of the Pilgrims of Plymouth Colony as the first characters in the first chapter of New England's Western history. But the fact is that this group appeared on the scene only after a remarkable succession of explorers and colonizers had already arrived and, for the most part, departed. It was the information supplied by these earlier pioneers that provided the body of knowledge that influenced these courageous religious immigrants to come here in the first place.

The New World had long held a fascination for European adventurers. John Cabot passed along the Newfoundland coast within a few years of Columbus' landing at San Salvador. And in all likelihood, Basque and Portugese fishermen plied the waters from Cape Cod to Newfoundland throughout the 1500s, harvesting the rich fisheries there and drying their fish on unnamed coasts. If so, such activities must have kept them very

land was owned in common, each person was expected to make a contribution. Specific tasks were assigned to those who showed aptitude for them; thus certain tribe members acquired special occupations—pottery- or arrow-making, for example.

These Indians settled Cape Cod sparsely, numbering only about two thousand, but they did exert a definite impact on the land. With fire as a tool, they burned the forests and the tangled undergrowth in their efforts to improve hunting and the berry harvest and to permit easier travel overland. Even so, when the European adventurers arrived Cape Cod still was covered almost entirely by forests.

Probing the New World

The waters are almost pure . . . the Herbs and Fruits are of many sorts and kinds. . . .

Oake is the chiefe wood . . . Firre, Pine, Wall-nut, Chesse-nut, Birtch, Ash, Elme, Cipris, Cedar, Mulbery, Plum tree, Hazell, Saxefras, . . .

Eagles . . . Hawkes . . . Geese, Brants, Cormorants, Ducks, Cranes, Swannes . . . Gulls, Turkies, Divedoppers, and many . . . whose names I know not.

Whales, Grompus, Porkpisces, Turbut, Sturgion, Cod, Hake, Haddocke. . . .

Moos . . . Deare . . . Bevers, Wolves, Foxes . . . wilde Cats, Beares, Otters, Martins. . . .

All these and divers other good things doe here for want of use still increase and decrease with little diminution.

—*John Smith's History of New England,* 1614

ELLIS HERWIG/IMAGE BANK

18

busy, since they apparently did not record their impressions of these sites.

There were many others who were more obliging to historians—a great list of explorers who came in small ships and recorded what they saw: Henry Hudson (1509), Giovanni da Verrazano (1524), Estevan Gomez (1525), Stephen Bellinger (1583), Martin Pring (1603), Sieur de Monts and his famous cartographer Samuel de Champlain (1605 and 1606), George Weymouth (1605), Captain John Smith (1614), Thomas Dermer (1619), and many, many more. Each one added to the growing store of knowledge about the northeastern coastline, its natural riches, and its Indian inhabitants.

The odd shape of Cape Cod early caught the notice of the cartographers of the day, who no doubt took pleasure in adding such a picturesque entity to their maps. The Cape, appearing on a number of charts (increasingly accurate as time went on), was labeled in a variety of ways, each reflecting its maker's view of the Cape as an extension of his own homeland. It was *Cap Blanc* (French), *Cape de Las Arenas* (Portuguese), *Staten Hoeck* (Dutch), and *Cape James* (English). But it was another English name, *Cape Cod*, that endured, appropriately coined in 1602 by one Bartholomew Gosnold, who found the bay waters to be rich in gigantic cod.

In reality, then, the Cape Cod area was not only already known prior to the arrival of the Pilgrims, it had been penetrated, explored, and described. Its riches, real or imagined, tantalized Europeans, and the tapping of these resources began a chain of activities here that in time would radically alter the landscape. For example, sassafras—an American product that was highly touted as a panacea for most ills—was for a time the rage

Oblivious to the golden sunlight that enshrines them, two clammers bend in unison over the fertile tidal flats.

Once a coveted item for export to the Old World, sassafras now is more valued as a bright touch of fall color.

of Europe. Gosnold himself carried a shipload of the medicinal bark from the Elizabeth Islands to England, as instructed by his financial backers, who thereupon sold the New World curative for 336 British pounds sterling per ton.

Contact with the Europeans had inevitably brought change to the American Indians, as they began to acquire new ways and new languages.

Unfortunately, the New World tribes also acquired Old World diseases. These were illnesses they had never known, the effects of which were often swift and tragic.

Between 1614 and 1619, a "plague" decimated coastal tribes. Four out of every five natives died, and populations of whole villages just disappeared. With the loss of these large numbers in such a short length of time, the tribes also lost most of their cultures.

Too few members were left to effectively resist the European encroachment and keep the old traditions alive. On the Lower Cape, from elbow to fingers, the Wampanoag population (estimated at about two thousand) was largely destroyed, and the tribe never recovered its former strength; by 1764 eleven Indians were left in Wellfleet, and four survived in Eastham! Only a few Wampanoag influences remain today on the Lower Cape to commemorate this once great people: some unploughed refuse heaps of shells marking former house sites, a scattering of Wampanoag place names (whose pronunciations are only distantly related to the Wampanoag language), and a few artifacts.

A symbol of colonial Cape Cod, this Eastham windmill grinds corn just as it did centuries ago. By the early 1800s, industrious settlers had built forty windmills on Cape Cod, in an effort to supply energy for their pre-petroleum society.

Ice-flecked waves, spawned by one of winter's powerful "no'eastas," churn toward a frozen shore.

SETTLEMENT AND COLONY LIFE

*. . . the whole countrie, full of woods & thickets,
represented a wild & savage [view]. If they looked
behind them, ther was the mighty ocean which they
had passed, and was now as a maine barr & goulfe
to seperate them from all the civill parts of the world.*

—WILLIAM BRADFORD
Of Plymouth Plantation, ca. 1630

The choice of Plymouth as a settlement site by the Pilgrims was one of those occurrences that, although accidental, nevertheless altered the course of history. The original destination of the colonists was the land that had been patented to them in the northern Virginia territory near the Hudson River. But the *Mayflower* almost foundered among treacherous shoals and roaring breakers while attempting to reach this destination by passing around the Cape's elbow, and the captain was forced to steer northward instead. After sailing around the great fist of Cape Cod, the ship laid anchor within its protecting harbor. The date was November 11, 1620, by the Pilgrims' calendar (November 21 by ours).

It is one of our most persistent historical myths that the Pilgrims' first contact with the New World was made at Plymouth Rock. In reality, the Pilgrims first set foot on the shores of the New World at the site that is now Provincetown. While the *Mayflower* rode in safety in Provincetown Harbor, the Pilgrims made discovery sallies along the coast by means of long boat and shallop.

Winter was threateningly close; the location for a settlement had to be decided, and quickly. The men of the *Mayflower,* led by Captain Myles Standish and aided by the ship's captain and crew, lost no time in exploring the Lower Cape, often on foot. Finally, upon the suggestion of the *Mayflower's* pilot, who knew the place from a previous voyage, the ship was brought into Plymouth Harbor. This was December 26 (new calendar), 1620, the beginning of the Plymouth Colony, the first successful English colony in New England.

But this success would not be achieved without incredible hardship and almost unendurable heartbreak. The *Mayflower* flock was forced to live between ship and land for most of that first dreadful winter, when exposure and disease took a toll of more than half their number. The next November the dwindling Plymouth population

Row upon row, rank cowlicks of salt-marsh hay add warmth and texture to salt-marsh scenes. The grass grows only in areas flooded at least twice monthly by spring tides.

Indeed, it could be argued that the colonists owed the success of their colonization efforts to Squanto and other friendly Indians, who taught them how to plant Indian corn and fertilize it, hunt the wild turkey and deer, and fish from the sea. The Pilgrims themselves knew well how much they were indebted to these strange new friends, who could have easily destroyed the vulnerable colony if they had so chosen.

What was life like in colony days? Well, we certainly know that it was arduous; an enormous amount of hard manual labor went into just providing the requirements of day-to-day living. But hard work was nothing new to the Pilgrims, who had already undergone years of exile in Holland. In this, and in all things, they quite naturally followed the traditions and habits learned in their English world. Dress, coinage, laws, architecture, techniques of agriculture—all were those of the land they had left far behind them, modified only by the circumstances in which they now found themselves. The separation from the mother country was only physical, after all. The colonists did not hesitate to pledge their allegiance to Charles I, and they continued to take a keen interest in what was happening in England, where most still had kinfolk. They had put their roots down forever in the *new* England, but how

was bolstered somewhat by friends and relatives who arrived aboard the ill-provisioned *Fortune.* This was the event that prompted the first Thanksgiving, in which the surviving colonists, new arrivals, and more than ninety of Chief Massasoit's Indians took part. It was a celebration, even though the settlers were well aware that now their meager food supplies must stretch even further.

Despite their dire circumstances, the Pilgrims did have good reason to be thankful, perhaps even more than they then realized. Providence had directed them to a site that was one of the few along the New England coast that had been cleared for planting and that possessed abundant salt-marsh hay for cattle. The clearing had been done by the Indians, who did not press their prior claims, a second bit of luck. And thirdly, the Indians among whom the Pilgrims found themselves proved to be peaceable and friendly. Incredibly, a number of the Indians could speak the settlers' own language! Theirs was a broken English learned through contact with fishermen and traders; but one of them—Squanto, who had been shanghaied, taken to England, and returned—spoke English fluently. (He later served the immigrants well as interpreter.)

often must they have yearned for the comforts and familiarity of the *old!*

The staunch religious beliefs held by the colonists were reflected in the Christian names of biblical origin that they gave their children: Patience and Deliverance, Mercy and Obadiah, Zacaryah and Job. But these were Pilgrims, not Puritans, and they enjoyed their fun, their spirits, and their individuality—no doubt more than the governing elders wished, if we can depend upon the evidence of the Plymouth court records:

> 1655: *It was Enacted That such as shall deney the Scriptures to bee a rule of life shall receive Corporall punishment according to the descretion of the Majestrate soe as it shall not extend to life or Limb.*
>
> 1657: *William Hailstone . . . fined, for two lyes told by him [in a court petition], the sume of twenty shillings.*
>
> 1659: *Samuell House is enjoyned by the Court to take some speedy course with a dogg that is troublesome and dangerouse in biting folkes as they goe by the highwaies.*
>
> 1679: *Joseph Peirse, for playing att cards once, fined ten shillings. Joseph Thorne, . . . for playing att cards twise, fined one pound.*

Of course, stocks and a whipping post were displayed permanently and prominently in town squares, in an effort to discourage such distressing and irreligious behavior.

The open land of Plymouth was large enough to accommodate the immediate agricultural needs of the Pilgrims. Soon, however, the steady influx of immigrants used up the readily available land, which was planted to crops of corn, rye, and wheat. Necessity led to invention, as it often does, and the Pilgrims were very resourceful indeed. They also sought out and utilized the marsh hay, so prevalent on the coast, as a natural and convenient source of fodder for cattle and one already familiar to these Englishmen.

Expanded settlement led to the establishment of new towns. Sandwich, with its broad marshes, was the first to be incorporated (1637), followed in quick succession by the towns of Yarmouth (1639), Barnstable (1639), and Eastham (1644). Each new freeman of the widespreading Plymouth Colony received twenty acres of land for his own use. So, year by year, the wilderness was pushed back as the new civilization grew.

And, year by year, the colonists came to rely

The delicate tracery of the Virginia creeper enhances swamp and woodland—and in autumn adds a splash of fiery red.

JOHN W. GREGORY

A Harwich church tower points symbolically heavenward. The richness of the architectural detail that is present in New England churches evolved in the seventeenth and eighteenth centuries.

more and more upon the sea. The *Mayflower* flock had come to the New World as farmers and thus was ill-prepared to take advantage of what the sea, now in such constant and close proximity, had to offer. So oriented to the land were the Pilgrims that there was not even one fishhook to be found among them!

But this was a new land and a new era. They, and the generations to follow, would soon learn that the *sea* was dominant here, and by it would they live—and perish.

SUGGESTED READING

BRADFORD, WILLIAM. *Of Plymouth Plantation, 1620–1647.* New York: Alfred A. Knopf, 1952.

KITTREDGE, HENRY C. *Cape Cod—Its People and Their People.* Second Ed. Boston, Mass.: Houghton Mifflin Co., 1968.

LEVERMORE, CHARLES. *Forerunners and Competitors of the Pilgrims and Puritans.* Brooklyn, New York: New England Soc. of Brooklyn, 1912.

WHIPPLE, CHANDLER. *The Indian and the White Man in Massachusetts and Rhode Island.* Stockbridge, Mass.: The Berkshire Traveller Press, 1973.

Overleaf: Unintimidated by the frantic dance of the waves, a lone sanderling gleans the Great Beach. Photo by Glenn Van Nimwegen

Harvesting the Seas

Cape Cod girls, they have no combs,
Heave away, heave away;
They comb their hair with codfish bones,
We are bound for Australia.

Cape Cod cats, they have no tails,
Heave away, heave away;
They blew away in heavy gales,
We are bound for Australia.

—From a sea chantey

The sea encloses and envelops Cape Cod, and it is its greatest heritage. As the colonist farmers came to understand and accept this, they learned to use the rich resources that were available in the sea, the marshes, and the tidal flats. Lobster and cod were astonishingly abundant, as were oysters, mussels, clams, crabs, and scallops. Herring and alewives were so common that the Pilgrims could actually scoop them from the waterways and use them liberally to fertilize their crops, as the Indians had taught them.

Still, fishing was largely part-time work, usually pursued in the wintertime or after the farming chores were done. This casual attitude did not extend to the drift whales that frequently washed up on the beaches, however. The new Cape Cod inhabitants quickly learned that the products to be derived from these whales could be turned to immediate profit. Disputes among citizens concerning claims on these carcasses became common, even to the point of creating real strife among citizens and towns and within the colonial government.

It was inevitable, given the profitability of "drift" whaling, that it would evolve into "shore" whaling, in which the minke, right, and blackfish (pilot) whales of Cape Cod Bay were actively pursued and slaughtered. "Try works" were built along the shores, in which whale blubber was rendered into oil. By 1740, the whales were gone from the bay, having been slaughtered or forced to abandon the now dangerous waters.

But whaling had become too important economically for the Cape Codders to be so easily discouraged, and they pursued the mammals farther and farther out to sea. "Deep-sea" whaling developed in this way, an industry that was carried on out of many Cape Cod towns, especially Provincetown, Truro, and Wellfleet. Eventually ships sailed to whaling grounds as far away as the South Pacific and the Arctic, on voyages that lasted up to as many as four years. Try works were built right into the decks of the whaling

Pursuing a time-honored way of life, this Wellfleet oysterman shucks away with a skill honed by years of practice. Cape Cod oysters are noted for their quality.

DAVID COATES

Nets and other fishing paraphernalia are the tools with which the Cape Cod fisherman reaps the crops of his aquatic farmland.

ships, and wood used for ballast served a double purpose since it later was burned under the try pots.

Nantucket and New Bedford both eventually eclipsed Cape Cod in whaling fame, but it was on Cape Cod that the industry began, and it was from here that the industry spread.

During the Revolutionary War, a British blockade of Cape Cod ports brought whaling to a virtual standstill, an economic disaster for these towns. Only Provincetown recovered to any degree. It continued its whaling tradition throughout the nineteenth century and until about 1916, when declining catches and the rise of the petroleum industry brought the whaling industry to an end there too.

Open-ocean fishing grew at a slower pace

Isolated in the fog, these cedar-sheathed fishing shacks huddle together on a shrouded shore. Cape Cod fishermen carry on their trade in all but the most severe weather; these humble shelters provide them with a minimum of comfort.

Whale watchers aboard the Dolphin III *are spellbound by the deep-sea performance of a humpback whale. Whales have long been an important resource in the economy of Cape Cod. Once relentlessly hunted for the profitable products to be derived from their carcasses, live whales (and porpoises) now contribute to the Cape's economy by attracting tourists. The Marine Mammal Act protects these important animals from hunting and harassment of any kind.*

CHARLES A. MAYO/PROVINCETOWN CENTER FOR COASTAL STUDIES

than whaling, but by the late colonial period, fishermen were plying their trade in the Grand Banks, off Newfoundland, in search of cod. From the Grand Banks, ships carried the fish to the West Indies, exchanged the catches for cargoes of rum and molasses, and returned home. It was a great triangle of trade that brought prosperity to many ports, especially Chatham, Harwich, and Barnstable.

These fleets dwindled during the Revolution, then rebounded rapidly as cod and mack-

erel began to be caught in even greater numbers. Banned from Canadian waters in 1818, fishermen began to learn how to fish the hazardous Georges Bank (a hundred miles east of the Cape) for cod and halibut; the ports of Provincetown, Truro, and Wellfleet reaped the benefits of the resulting profits.

In 1853, the newly developed "purse" seine made it possible to catch surface schools of mackerel, replacing the tedious process of "handlining" them, and boom years came to Cape Cod

ports. During the early 1850s, more than a hundred cod ships regularly jammed the Wellfleet harbor; Provincetown Harbor sheltered just as many, in addition to its huge fleet of mackerel schooners. Forests of masts were a daily scene in these harbors. So were the rows and rows of salted cod, drying in the sun.

By this time the Cape had completely metamorphosed. It was now a land of mariners. The soil was nearly gone; fishing, whaling, and trade with the Orient were now the principal means by which to earn a living. One generation after another followed the family tradition of going to sea.

But gradually Cape Cod lost ground to competing fishing ports. Seines and trawls—gear necessary for ships involved in the fishing industry—required capital, and lots of it. Furthermore, the Cape's shallow ports could not handle the larger steam-powered ships that were coming into use. Nor could the marketing convenience of a New Bedford or Gloucester be matched. The sight of the graceful, picturesque schooners grad-

ually faded and disappeared in harbor after harbor. The heyday was over. Only Provincetown, with its deep-water harbor, continued to be an important fishing center. It functioned as a major port until the end of the 1800s and still harbors an active fishing fleet.

Another common feature of the Cape Cod landscape disappeared along with the fishing boats—the salt vats that dotted the bay shore and marshes, where fish were salted preparatory to marketing, a process that required tons of salt. Salt-making by boiling seawater had been practiced in the colonial years, but it was the innovative Cape Cod solar vats that allowed salt to be produced on a large scale—a scale so tremendous that it effectively created another industry. By 1830, salt production had peaked. With 442 salt works operating on Cape Cod, the vats and their water-pumping windmills had become a familiar part of virtually every Cape Cod town. But when the inland salt mines opened, this enterprise, too, faded away.

Shipwrecks and Sea Rescue

Semper Paratus (Always Ready)
—Official Motto, U.S. Life Saving Service

You gotta go—
but you don't have to come back!
—Unofficial Motto, U.S. Life Saving Service

From the beginning of its history in the exploration and settlement of the New World, Cape Cod has been a mariner's nightmare. It is the burial place of some three thousand ships that throughout the years have wrecked upon its rugged shores or have sunk in its often tempestuous waters. The *Mayflower* itself almost foundered on Pollock's Rip, and three years afterward, Nauset Beach claimed the *Sparrowhawk,* in the first recorded wreck.

Shallow bars reach deceptively far offshore. And shoals, those remnants of once-exposed land, often lie treacherously just below the water's surface. But in the early years of New England's history, the seas were the only highways

RICHARD C. KELSEY

Flying against an ominous sky from a mast at Chatham's Coast Guard Station, full hurricane flags and hurricane lamps, coded red-white-red, issue a seldom-seen and urgent warning. Flags are rarely used in today's world.

HENRY K. CUMMINGS/COURTESY SNOW LIBRARY, ORLEANS, MASS.

On June 10, 1897, the Canadian schooner Walter Miller, *laden with lumber, grounded on Nauset Beach in Orleans, becoming another statistic on the long roster of Cape Cod shipwrecks.*
In the days of sail, all ships were at the mercy of the weather, unpredictable and capricious.

From 1923 until 1981 Nauset Light blinke
a three-flash code that carried on the tradition c
three separate lights first built here in 183?
Today's light flashes an alternating red-and-whit
pattern. The lens shown here is on exhibit a
Salt Pond Visitor Cente

of commerce available, and all trade that transpired between the busy ports of Boston and New York had to pass Cape Cod.

Time meant money, of course, and so the temptation was always great for a captain to cut corners in order to make time between the two ports. But these sailing vessels could perform only with the cooperation of the weather, and they were often handicapped by severe storms and heavy fog. Without adequate weather forecasting, no trip could be considered safe until it was over; howling New England gales could appear within minutes and mercilessly drive a hapless ship to its destruction. And no human being could survive the body-numbing waters of the North Atlantic for more than a few minutes; many a man, woman, and child died of exposure, even if he had managed to reach the shore somehow.

As Cape Codders turned more and more to fishing as a livelihood, shipwrecks occurred in increasing numbers. Inevitably, family after family lost a man—and often all of them—in a single gale. It was heartbreakingly common after a storm to see a shattered ship lying partially buried on a beach or marooned on a sandbar, agonizingly close to shore.

Concern for the victims of such disasters at last found expression in the efforts of the Massachusetts Humane Society, one of the world's earliest organized efforts at sea rescue. Beginning in 1786, this group of volunteers constructed straw-filled huts on remote beaches, in the hope that shipwrecked survivors might at least find temporary refuges from the weather. Guides to the locations of these shelters were distributed to sailors, who it was felt might someday have need of the life-sustaining structures. But in reality the success of this measure was minimal, and lives continued to be lost as the huts deteriorated and fell into ruins.

A more effective lifesaving measure was the many lighthouses that sprang up on Cape Cod, built in the hope of warning weather-blinded ships of imminent danger. In 1797 the first Highland Light, which burned whale oil as a beacon,

DAVID COATES

Resembling a giant shore nautilus, the steel stairway of Nauset Light sweeps upward in an artistic spiral. The thick brick walls represent an attempt at permanence by the lighthouse builders.

ED ELVIDGE

This monument to father and son, reminder of the harsh marine heritage of the Cape, tells the story of the loss at sea of a son of tender age. This is but one of many such tragedies documented in Cape Cod cemeteries.

With more than six hundred thousand candlepower, the double bullseye electric lamps of Highland Light—one of the most powerful lights on the Atlantic Coast—project a glow that is visible from more than thirty-two miles at sea on a clear day. Towering above the lighthouse is a radio beacon station, the latest and most efficient technological means of warning mariners of their position. Its signals are received hundreds of miles out at sea.

was built. Other lighthouses that warned of Cape Cod's dangerous beaches and shoals during the early nineteenth century were the Chatham Light (1808), the first Race Point Light (1816), Long Point (1826), and the original three Nauset lights (1838). By century's end, eleven kerosene or electric lighthouses stood watch along the Cape's ocean and bay shore, from elbow to fingertip.

During this era, many a wreck was picked clean of its salvageable remains by those who first happened along the shore. This was considered a legitimate way to earn a living, at least by those who lived in the area. There are some stories of "mooncussers," thieves who used false lights to lure ships to their destruction and then harvested the flotsam and jetsam, but these stories are probably no more than myth. No mooncussing has ever been proved; no mooncusser has ever been caught.

The great loss of life continued here and

Coastguardsmen inspect the workings of Wood End Light. The beacon flashes red every ten seconds, identifying its location—on the knuckles of Cape Cod's giant fist.

along other coastlines until 1871, when Congress was finally moved to create the United States Life Saving Service. Within a year, nine stations had been built on the Great Beach, and by the end of the century another four stations had been built. Together they provided thorough coverage of the high-hazard ocean beaches that stretched from Long Point to Monomoy Point.

Living at each station were a keeper and a crew of six or seven surfmen whom the keeper had trained with military precision in the techniques of sea rescue by surf boat or breeches buoy. From August 1 to June 1 of each year, the surfmen patrolled the beaches at night and during furious storms and thick, blanketing fog in search of wrecks, victims, and survivors. And each year, during the storm season, these intrepid men responded to as many as two dozen wrecks, perhaps saving as many as a hundred or more lives. These were the "Life Savers" of Cape Cod, men whose heroic deeds and unwavering devotion to duty gave them lasting fame and a well-deserved place in history.

Indeed, lifesaving continued to be a major Cape Cod occupation for fifty years or so. The same family names that had appeared in the earliest records of colonial settlement reappeared a century later on station rosters. And, as with fishing families, son followed father into a hazardous but very honorable career.

Gradually, however, the introduction of steam-powered ships and much more effective weather-forecasting methods reduced the element of chance in marine travel, and shipwrecks became less frequent. The long-dreamed-of Cape Cod Canal opened in 1914, and the merchant marine no longer had to pass the shoal- and bar-covered gauntlet off Cape Cod.

In 1915, the service combined with the Revenue Cutter Service and the Lighthouse Service to become the U.S. Coast Guard. One by one, the stations of the Life Saving Service fell into disuse and were abandoned; none operated after World War II. Only Old Harbor Station, which has been moved to Race Point Beach, survives intact, a reminder of the important role the U.S. Life Saving Service once played on Cape Cod.

The Coast Guard continues to operate on Cape Cod. With its powerful boats out of Chatham and Provincetown and its helicopters out of Otis Air Force Base in Mashpee and Sandwich, the Coast Guard now speedily accomplishes the routine chores and often heroic deeds that the courageous Life Savers of Cape Cod once so arduously performed.

NPS PHOTO

SUGGESTED READING

DALTON, J. W. *The Life Savers of Cape Cod.* Boston, Mass.: Barta Press, 1902. Reprinted by The Chatham Press, Old Greenwich, Conn.

QUINN, WILLIAM. *Shipwrecks Around Cape Cod.* Farmington, Maine: Knowlton & McLeary, 1973.

Juxtaposed incongruously against the great, windswept Atlantic surf, a weatherbeaten Cape Cod cottage clings to the barren dunes. The contrast of man-made and natural features is a common sight at Cape Cod, serving to create the distinctive landscapes that are instantly recognized as Cape Cod.

The house design originated on the Cape, where—in its eminently practical way—it has for centuries provided warmth during New England's icy winters and allowed for easy expansion as family sizes increased. Many Cape Cod houses that were built in the eighteenth and nineteenth centuries still survive, historic landmarks that are as important to preserve as the natural settings in the park. More than eighty privately owned houses within the boundaries of Cape Cod National Seashore are listed on the Historic American Buildings Survey. The houses will remain under private ownership.

Cape Cod Today

The overriding concern of the first settlers of Cape Cod was, of course, whether the new land could be made to yield all the materials they would need for daily living. English ships were infrequent, and few European products ever reached the colony. The colonists, accustomed as they were to an old and highly civilized environment, saw the New World (in the words of William Bradford) as a "hideous and desolate wilderness." It challenged and threatened their very existence: If they could not turn its resources—the only ones they had—to their own advantage, they would surely perish.

It was with this single-minded purpose that the settlers utilized all that the land, forests, and sea had to offer, making such demands on these resources that the face of Cape Cod soon was radically changed. It was a story that was to be repeated all across America.

Theirs was a pre-petroleum world. Energy had to come from elsewhere. Windmills provided the energy to grind grain where running water was lacking, but most of the settlers' needs drew heavily upon the forests. This included daily homemaking needs: A colonial family, for example, might use some forty cords of wood each year for heating, cooking, and washing.

As local industries grew, the forests provided material for every conceivable use: Wood was burned to boil sea water for salt and to render whale blubber into oil; trees became fences, poles, posts, and houses; lumber became boards, boxes, and barrels; pitch-pine tar yielded turpentine (the beginning of the naval-stores industry in this country); and whole forests were burned to yield potash for fertilizer, soapmaking, and glassmaking.

In 1656, the Plymouth government passed laws demanding the home manufacture of textiles, with fines for those families who did not weave a certain quota of woolen goods or lining cotton. Thus it was that sheep came to play an important part in the economy of the Lower Cape, at least for a while. Within twenty-seven years, the harm caused by these "hooved locusts" had become serious enough to prompt the passage of laws that would control them (among the earliest of the conservation laws to be enacted in the United States).

WILLIAM QUINN

As the principal recreation land for New England, Cape Cod hosts millions of visitors each year. Boating is one of its most exhilarating activities, as evidenced by these Pleasant Bay sailors.

A quahogger examines her sea harvest—with perhaps the same pleasure that settler and Indian experienced before her.

THE SLIDE INTO POVERTY

The country from Sandwich to Barnstable was hilly, and in a great degree bare, bleak, and desolate; the inhabitants having universally cut down their forests and groves, and taken no measures to renew them.

—TIMOTHY DWIGHT
    Travels in New-England and New-York, 1822

The land was not the only resource to feel the effects of heavy use. The forests that had greeted the colonists on their arrival at Cape Cod now began to dwindle as they were used to meet the increasing demands of the shipbuilding industry. During the early 1700s, as the colonists turned more and more to the sea, some 150 ships were built each year throughout the Massachusetts colony—with and without the approval of the king. And on Cape Cod, oaks ten to fifty inches in diameter were regularly cut down to satisfy the needs of the fishing, whaling, and trade industries. The King's Navy also required a share, and the best white pine was reserved for masts for its ships. Oaks for ship keels and ribs were loaded whole onto special ships and transported across the ocean to English shipyards.

It was not surprising, therefore, that the forests quickly gave out. By 1775, few trees were left on a land that originally had been heavily forested. Driftwood and peat from the marshes and swamps now became the principal sources for heating fuel. Even so, over the next century the remaining Cape Cod forests provided wood to fuel railroad steam engines and the Sandwich Glass Works, and they provided charcoal to fuel the bog iron furnaces that flourished between Dennis and Plymouth. Cape Cod forests even

provided the fuel that heated the homes of far-away Boston.

Not everyone was blind to the decimation of the forests and the abuse of the land. The concerns of a few are reflected in some of the laws that appear on colonial books. For example: During the 1670s, indiscriminate logging was forbidden in Eastham. In 1714, the people of Pamet were offered twenty-five shillings each to build fences to control cattle grazing.

But throughout the years such measures, though frequent, were not very far-reaching. Early travelers and local historians describe the steady deterioration of the land:

1745: *Blowing sand a continuous menace.*

1809: *[Yarmouth] a sea of sand.*

1822: *Practically no fuel on the Outer Cape.*
In Eastham the surface . . . a perfect plain.

1839: *The soil, for the most part . . . but a barren waste of sand.*

1850: *A large part of the real estate [Orleans] freely moving back and forth in the air.*

1855: *Not . . . worth writing a deed for.*

With human encroachment and the resultant loss of habitats, many animals also disappeared from the Cape Cod scene. The wolf, bear, gray fox, and coyote were eradicated locally, as was the native turkey. Massive market hunting all along the Atlantic Coast during the last half of

Picturesque Province-town ("P-town" to locals) turns its back to the land and faces the sea, appropriately enough since it owes its fame as a seaport to the deep-water whaling and fishing of yester-year. The fishing tradi-tion continues, although tourism has replaced it as the town's principal industry. In summer, when travelers seek the charm and flavor of the old port, Provincetown's popula-tion swells tenfold.

In a scene once but no longer common, a harvester of Cape Verdean ancestry helps gather the cranberry crop by hand. Mechanical harvesters are now widely used to perform this chore.

workers and their families to join the farmers in the movement West. Cape Cod had arrived at its biological and economic low.

THE SLOW RECOVERY

In autumn, even in August, the thoughtful days begin, and we can walk anywhere with profit.
—HENRY DAVID THOREAU, *Cape Cod,* 1855

The New England climate is generally kind to the land. Rainfall is evenly distributed through-out the year; and the earth, if not abused, is readily reforested. When the wholesale exploita-tion of its resources finally stopped, Cape Cod began such a recovery, as did much of New Eng-land, and this recovery is still going on. By the end of the nineteenth century, bearberry had begun to carpet the barren ground; eastern red cedar had begun to invade old fields; Atlantic white cedar and red maple had reappeared in some of the swamps.

To speed up the process of reclamation, thou-sands of acres of moving sand were planted, dur-ing the late 1800s, with pitch pine. It is true that

the nineteenth century virtually eliminated the last populations of most coastal birds: The once common heath hen became extinct; so did the great auk, passenger pigeon, and Labrador duck.

It was inevitable that the uncontrolled use of the resources of Cape Cod would eventually re-sult in the decline of its industries. This began to happen during the last half of the nineteenth century, primarily because of the loss of fuel, soil, and other natural resources. Industries such as salt, wool, glass, iron, fishing, and whaling all felt the effects. The decline of these once-strong economic entities—together with the increasing competition of the China trade—forced many

Rich Corinthian columns, dentil work, and a mansard roof embellish the French Second Empire home constructed over a century ago by Eastham's Captain Edward Penniman, who went to sea at the age of eleven. Many sea captains, enriched by whaling and the China trade, built similarly elegant homes as visible symbols of their successes.

today the great parabolic dunes of the Province Lands still claim the areas where Pilgrims once found oak-pine forests, but there are now more forests on Cape Cod than at any time in the past three centuries.

A bright spot, both literally and figuratively, in the Cape's economic fortunes was its cranberries. *Sassamanesh*, the Wampanoags called the tart fruit that served as both food and medicine to them. We usually associate Thanksgiving with the Plymouth Colony, but Cape Cod is also linked with this tradition, for it was here that this indis-

pensable holiday fruit was first harvested for commercial use.

The "crane berry," a native plant, commonly grew on the wet, sandy soils of Cape Cod. For decades, however, the colonists could gather only sparse and unpredictable crops of the low-growing fruit. Then, in the early 1800s, a Dennis resident observed that yields of the berry increased after nature had covered the bogs with blowing sand. Using a similar but artificial sanding technique, Cape Codders turned to the bogs, as they once had turned to the sea, and the enterprise for which Cape Cod is most famous was born.

A family of the 1840s could earn $200 to $400 each year from every acre they could plant, a prospect that caused virtually every former red-maple and Atlantic-white-cedar swamp, long since cut-over and "worthless," to be converted into cranberry bogs. Most fields were developed in the area west of Orleans; a few bogs appeared north of the elbow. By century's end, Barnstable County led the state in the production of this remarkable fruit.

Many regions of the nation now surpass this area in cranberry production. But in the public mind, Cape Cod and cranberries remain inseparable, and this bright berry is still a distinctive part of the Cape Cod scene.

A New Industry: Tourism

The time must come when this coast will be a place of resort for those New-Englanders who really wish to visit the sea-side. At present it is wholly unknown to the fashionable world, and probably it will never be agreeable to them.

—Henry David Thoreau, *Cape Cod*, 1855

Cape Cod, even in its most poverty-stricken years, has always been the object of exploration by curious and observant travelers, however few and far-between. During much of the nineteenth

Another reminder of the Cape's marine heritage are these whale jawbones, which frame an old schoolhouse (of Greek Revival style), now a museum.

Houses of yesterday can be readily distinguished—by the discerning—from their modern architectural counterparts. This "full Cape" was constructed in the 1700s: Its front windows, which are twelve-pane over twelve-pane, are high on the wall, against the eaves. The placement and huge size of the chimney indicate that a multiple fireplace resides within—as well as a beehive oven.

century, travel was arduous—beyond Sandwich it had to be done on foot or by stagecoach—and the area was little publicized. However, as writers such as Henry David Thoreau, Thomas Kendall, and Timothy Dwight began to publish their descriptions of Cape Cod and Cape Codders in the popular magazines of the day, East Coast readers became more knowledgeable about the area. Many were intrigued by its uniqueness and yearned to see Cape Cod for themselves.

Also, the rails, by 1869, had at last reached Provincetown. In an effort to promote rail travel and shipping, the Old Colony Railroad began to promote the Cape. Tourism grew steadily in the last quarter of the century, and Americans came in increasing numbers to observe the distinctive Cape Codder way of life, to see the spectacular beauty of the Cape Cod landscapes, and to enjoy the wealth of history offered by the Cape. Summer cottages began to dot the scene, serving the lucky few would could stay for an entire season.

So, although Cape Cod had been left in an economic backwater as America entered the industrial age, the heritage of its gracious and gallant way of life was not all lost in the tides of change.

One of the most visible of these traditions on Cape Cod is its buildings, and it is to this architectural heritage that Cape Cod owes much of its flavor and character. Many a Cape Cod village is graced with elegant houses of Federal, Georgian, Greek Revival, and French Second Empire design, reminders of the sea captains and the prosperous days of fishing, whaling, and the China trade.

All of these styles had considerable impact on America as it moved westward. But it is the lowly Cape Cod house that has had the most lasting and far-reaching architectural influence on the nation.

The Cape Cod house had its origins in English ideals of architecture, but between 1700 and 1850 it had so evolved—in response to local needs and ideas—that it had become a truly unique expression of the Cape. Variations on this distinctive style were commonly referred to as a "half Cape" (two windows to one side of the front door); a "three-quarter Cape" (two windows to one side of the door, one window on the other); and a "full Cape" (two windows to each side of the door). These fractional descriptions often reflected the gradual expansion of a home throughout generations of occupancy.

In a dazzling display of amber and gold, creations of pressed, molded, and blown Sandwich glass glorify a window. The Sandwich Glass Works, established in 1825, did not use native sand but instead imported a distant earthen variety. The loss of local sources of wood, used for fuel, prompted the demise of the company in 1888, but the firm's products continue to be highly cherished.

Efficient and economical in design, the ground-hugging Cape Cod house became a Cape trademark, an intrinsic part of that elusive attraction we recognize as "charm." So, too, were Cape Cod's windswept fields and dunes, waterwheels and windmills and cemeteries, and the countless local vignettes of fishing and village life.

Drawn by these picturesque attractions and by the unsurpassed quality of the "light," turn-of-the-century painters arrived in Provincetown virtually en masse. By 1916 there were five art schools in the village; by 1920 Provincetown was one of the major creative centers of the nation.

The beach provides relaxation for people of all ages.

The works and teachings of such prominent artists of the day as Ambrose Webster, Charles Hawthorne, and Hans Hoffman attracted many likewise-talented people. The artistic flavor that permeated Provincetown during this period pervades the atmosphere of the town yet today.

Writers, too, were drawn here, perhaps not only by the charm but by the simplicity and independence of the Cape Cod way of life. Such early-twentieth-century geniuses in American literature as Eugene O'Neill and Edmund Wilson became a part of that life, adding to the Cape's growing fame and stature in the arts.

So, by the 1920s, Cape Cod was well known as a tourist destination, easily accessible by car. Recreation was now the Cape's major industry, a position that it holds with even more authority today, as travel to the Cape continues to increase from year to year. Tourists come in fall to see the autumnal tints and graceful migrating birds; in winter to watch the surf pounding with dramatic intensity on desolate beaches; in spring to observe the tender wildflowers and to reap the bounteous harvests of the fleet; and in summer to enjoy a multitude of activities (surf-fishing, theater-going, clamming, boating, hiking), to participate in the generous berry harvest, or just to observe the ever-changing landscape that embraces land and sea, forest and marsh, beach and meadow.

The Making of a Park

By 1938 the popularity of Cape Cod was so great that it became the focus of an attempt to create a national park. It was a noble idea, but it died quickly in the turmoil and larger concerns of World War II.

It was not until 1955 that the Lower Cape again claimed the conservationists' attention, having been identified by the National Park Service as one of the major recreational resources of the Atlantic Coast. It was a distinction well deserved: Cape Cod was within a two-day drive of one-third of the American population. Moreover, lying as it did that close to the densely settled Northeast, it was readily accessible to a region that was critically short of public recreation land. Several Congressional bills were introduced in an effort to create a national seashore, but still no action was forthcoming.

It was inevitable that such a proposal would cause controversy, for its adoption would mean that land that had been lived on for three centuries, often by the same families, would become part of the public domain. Feelings of heritage are strong on Cape Cod, and there were those who saw the proposal as a rude intrusion in a way of life that Cape families had enjoyed for centuries. Others saw it as a "take-over" by outsiders or, worse, by the federal government, an entity frequently distrusted by self-reliant New Englanders.

But a rapid wave of development was enveloping the seacoasts, and it became more and

PETER SIMON/BLACK STAR

Since the turn of the century, Cape Cod has been a haven for writers and painters, who in turn have given it national prominence.

more apparent to concerned people that without some form of protection the fate of the Lower Cape was all too predictable. What was once worthless land was being subdivided at a rapid rate.

Concern for the future of Cape Cod finally won out. In September of 1959, Massachusetts

With youthful glee, two boys abandon themselves to the frothy surf of Cape Cod's Great Beach. Created to meet the pressing leisure-time needs of the populous Northeast, Cape Cod National Seashore has become a major recreational asset.

Parents and children share in the excitement of fishing from shore for striped bass and bluefish.

Senators John F. Kennedy and Leverett Saltonstall introduced a revised bill. And, after many a stormy town meeting, public hearing, compromise, and boundary revision, Cape Cod National Seashore became a reality. On August 7, 1961, Kennedy himself, now president, signed the park into law.

It was the culmination of a concerted effort by many people, including Massachusetts Natural Resource Commissioners Francis W. Sargent, Charles Foster, Arthur T. Lyman, and the editors and contributors to the local weekly *The Cape Codder*. Without such support, the park proposal would surely have died.

The park included all of the Great Beach from Long Point in Provincetown to the southern tip of Nauset Beach in Chatham. It included inland woods, swamps, rivers, marshes, and bayside beaches.

In one respect, particularly, Cape Cod was a park quite unlike any other: The legislation that created the park allowed the continuation of some of the recreational activities—swimming, hunting, clamming, hiking—that were traditional in the area. These activities, however, were henceforth to be pursued in such a way that the unique flora and fauna of the Cape Cod seashore would

Cape Cod landscapes are low and wide and distant. Water and sky seem to emphasize the inconsequence and impermanence of man's embellishments.

Sport fishermen return at dusk to a safe harbor.

be there for future generations also to enjoy.

An advisory commission was created, which gave the six towns of the Lower Cape a chance to participate in park development. A "grandfather clause" gave to bona-fide homeowners—those who had possession as of September 1, 1959 (when the park bill was first introduced)—the right to remain in their homes and to sell or pass them on to whomever they chose. The bill also specified that park development would be carried out in a way that would "not diminish for its owners or occupants the value or enjoyment of any improved property."

The purpose, then, was not to create a wilderness, but to continue the recreational activities the area already accommodated, to halt development, and to perpetuate the rural, historic, and natural scenes that travelers had come here to enjoy in the first place. The flood of humanity that now inundates Cape Cod suggests what the land might have become had private and commercial development been allowed to proceed at an unchecked rate.

Ardent conservationists did not view the park legislation as all that they had hoped for, allowing as it did uses not entirely compatible with the philosophy of the National Park Service, which traditionally aims at conservation and protection through a *no-use* policy. However, the availability of public land located next to urban regions of the nation was becoming more and more restricted; therefore, the multiple-use character of this park was recognized as the shape of things to come in parks of the future. And in spite of the heavy use it sees each year, Cape Cod National Seashore continues to carry out the purpose of conservation, which in this instance is the preservation of *historic* and *natural* resources as well as the wise use of *recreational* and *social* values.

There are growing pains. A park that receives over five million visitors each year is bound to have them. These problems, although not unique to this area, are indicative of those that many parks will face in the decades ahead, when the pressures of use will increase, perhaps even becoming larger than we can now envision.

How, for example, can ponds—and their fresh-water quality—be protected while still serving the needs of huge numbers of visitors? How can hunting be accommodated without compromising the aims of conservation? How can the privileges of private homeowners and the public be simultaneously protected? How can the use of over-sand vehicles be allowed without endangering the ecosystems of nature and without undermining the more spiritual and aesthetic experiences that many people seek here? Such are the questions that unavoidably confront the administrators of this park—and of any park wherein the goals of both preservation and use are indicated. Equally challenging, here at Cape Cod, is the question of how to adapt to an ever-retreating coastline.

SUGGESTED READING

BESTON, HENRY. *The Outermost House*. New York: Ballantine, 1971.

BURROWS, FREDRIKA A. *Cannonballs and Cranberries*. Taunton, Mass.: William S. Sullwold, 1976.

DOANE, DORIS. *A Book of Cape Cod Houses*. Riverside, Conn.: The Chatham Press, 1970.

LEONARD, JOHNATHAN NORTON. *The Atlantic Beaches*. New York: Time-Life, 1976.

SECKLER, DOROTHY. *Provincetown Painters, 1890s–1970s*. Syracuse, New York: Everson Museum of Art, 1977.

STRAHLER, ARTHUR N. *Cape Cod Viewed from Santa Barbara*. Orleans, Mass.: Assn. for the Preservation of Cape Cod, 1973.

THOMSON, BETTY FLANDERS. *The Changing Face of New England*. New York: The Macmillan Co., 1958.

THOREAU, HENRY DAVID. *Cape Cod*. New York: Thomas Y. Crowell, 1966.

On a bayside shore, in the waning light of a summer evening, two children are joined in an enchanted spell. Nearby is the place where the Pilgrims, exploring the Cape in 1620, first encountered the Indians. In this land, settled as it has been for three and a half centuries, virtually every acre has a story to be told.

JOHN SCHRAM

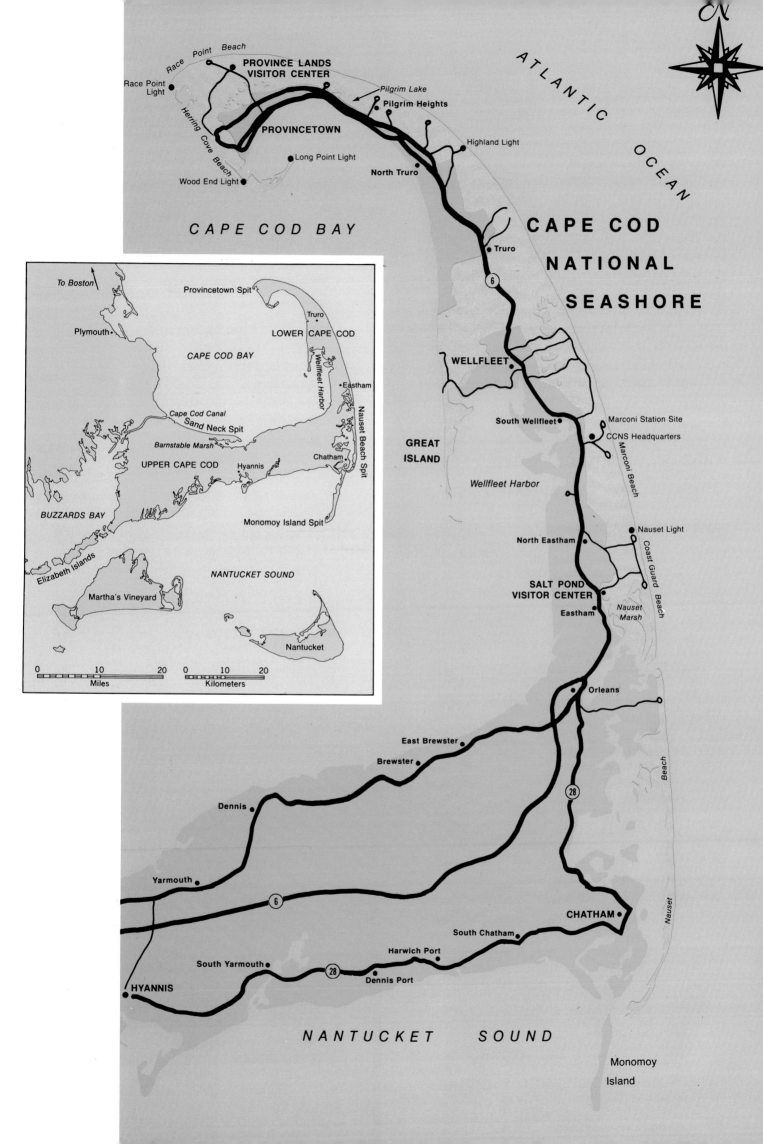

ATLANTIC OCEAN

Race Point Beach
PROVINCE LANDS VISITOR CENTER
Race Point Light
Pilgrim Lake
Pilgrim Heights
Herring Cove Beach
PROVINCETOWN
Highland Light
Long Point Light
North Truro
Wood End Light

CAPE COD BAY

CAPE COD NATIONAL SEASHORE

Truro
6

WELLFLEET

GREAT ISLAND

South Wellfleet
Marconi Station Site
CCNS Headquarters

Wellfleet Harbor

Marconi Beach

Nauset Light

North Eastham

SALT POND VISITOR CENTER
Coast Guard Beach

Eastham
Nauset Marsh

Orleans

East Brewster

Brewster

28

Dennis

Beach

Yarmouth

6

CHATHAM

South Chatham

Harwich Port

South Yarmouth
28
Dennis Port
HYANNIS

Nauset

NANTUCKET SOUND

Monomoy Island

To Boston

Provincetown Spit
Truro
Plymouth
LOWER CAPE COD

CAPE COD BAY
Wellfleet Harbor

Cape Cod Canal
Sand Neck Spit
Eastham

Barnstable Marsh
Nauset Beach Spit

UPPER CAPE COD
Hyannis
Chatham

BUZZARDS BAY

NANTUCKET SOUND

Monomoy Island Spit

Elizabeth Islands

Martha's Vineyard

Nantucket

0	10	20
Miles

0	10	20
Kilometers

The Heritage of Cape Cod

If we have learned anything from our experiences at Cape Cod National Seashore, it is an acute awareness of just how fragile the land really is. Yet, even with the heavy impact that great use puts upon it, Cape Cod continues its biologic recovery. Forests of oak and pine are becoming more and more abundant; fields of wildflowers are expanding their borders; birds are populating forests, marsh, and shore in increasing numbers and varieties. And the very nature of the park constitutes a continually growing source of instruction, pleasure, and inspiration.

All of these benefits go as deep and will last as long as its immensely valuable historic aspects. At least as deep and long-lasting should be our regard for this park, for it is we who are here in the present who will determine what the quality of this park will be for our descendants. Cape Cod National Seashore, with all its remarkable restorative powers and with all the richness and substance it contributes to our heritage, is a national treasure. If generations of our children can feel and see and respond to this place as we are able now to do, then we have passed on a legacy that is very, very precious indeed.

As Americans, living in a democracy, we are not obliged to seek freedom from human despots by leaving a beloved homeland, as our Pilgrim ancestors once did. But the struggle to achieve and retain the freedom and dignity of the soul is a never-ending one. So it is still a principle—and, one might argue, the *same* principle—that brings us as well to these New England shores.

In the shifting sands and fragile beauty of this Cape Cod landscape lies a heritage that is strong and impressive, and a vision that is awesome. Perhaps *just* as awesome is the responsibility we bear to pass this heritage and this vision on to those who in the future will stand upon these shores—a mere three hundred years from now and in the countless centuries beyond.

NICHOLAS DEVORE III/BRUCE COLEMAN INC.

Gulls and a lonely pier are silhouetted in a golden, summer-morning mist.

Quiet moments on a quiet sea are a fitting end to summer. NPS photo

Back cover: A trail in winter-colored beachgrass leads to the meeting place of land, sky, and water. Photo by David Coate

Books in this series: Acadia, Alcatraz Island, Arches, Blue Ridge Parkway, Bryce Canyon, Canyon de Chelly, Cape Cod, Capitol Reef, Channel Islands, Civil War Parks, Crater Lake, Death Valley, Denali, Dinosaur, Everglades, Fort Clatsop, Gettysburg, Glen Canyon–Lake Powell, Grand Canyon, Grand Teton, Great Smoky Mountains, Haleakala, Hawaii Volcanoes, Lake Mead–Hoover Dam, Lincoln Parks, Mount Rainier, Mount Rushmore, Mount St. Helens, National Park Service, Olympic, Petrified Forest, Rocky Mountain, Sequoia–Kings Canyon, Scotty's Castle, Shenandoah, Theodore Roosevelt, Virgin Islands, Yellowstone, Yosemite, Zion

Published by KC Publications · Box 14883 · Las Vegas, NV 89114

Printed by Dong-A Printing Co., Ltd., Seoul, Korea
Separations by Color Masters